THE
HONEY HEALING
KITCHEN:

51 Honey-Infused Recipes to Nourish, Strengthen and Heal Your Body

ALTERNATIVE
DAILY

TABLE OF CONTENTS

SWEET TREATS:

DRINKS:

INTRODUCTION

Cooking with honey is a pleasure and a privilege. Not only is honey loaded with healing properties, but it tastes great, too. That's why we call it liquid gold!

Honey is an especially wonderful gift for sweet and savory cooking and baking. The best way to incorporate honey into your kitchen (and your medicine chest) is to purchase local honey or certified organic honey.

You've probably heard that honeybees are in trouble… and supporting your local beekeeper is a win-win-win situation. You win because you get high-quality honey. The beekeeper wins because they get support for their small business. And the bees win because small local producers take much better care of their bees than huge honey corporations.

It is worth the little extra you may pay for the peace of mind that your honey is actually honey, and not some artificially sweetened honey-colored liquid that could be contaminated with herbicides, pesticides, and other toxins. Research demonstrates that raw honey has the most potent medicinal benefits and is loaded with nutrients, antioxidants, and valuable enzymes.

Happy, healthy, and sweet cooking!

GET-UP-AND-GO OATMEAL ENERGY BALLS

*These healthy oatmeal balls are a great start to your day,
or a nutritious anytime snack.*

Total Time: 45 minutes, plus 3 hours to chill
Servings: about 24 balls

INGREDIENTS

1 ½ cups rolled gluten-free oats

½ cup wheat germ (substitute flax seed to make it gluten-free)

½ cup dried dates

½ cup sunflower seeds

½ cup chia seeds

½ cup peanut butter

½ cup honey

2 tablespoons orange marmalade

INSTRUCTIONS

1. Line a baking pan with wax paper.

2. Mix oats, wheat germ or flax, dates, and half of the sunflower and chia seeds in a food processor. Pulse a few times until blended.

3. Add peanut butter, honey, and marmalade. Mix until combined and the dough forms a ball.

4. Chill for 30 minutes.

5. Finely chop the remaining sunflower kernels and chia seeds together.

6. With wet hands, make bite-sized balls with the chilled mixture and roll in the sunflower and chia seed mixture.

7. Place the finished balls on the baking sheet and return to the refrigerator to chill for a few hours.

8. Store the balls in an airtight container for up to a week.

HONEY-NUT GRANOLA

*Enjoy this granola for breakfast or for a
naturally sweet snack anytime.*

Total Time: 1 hour, 15 mins
Servings: 6-8

INGREDIENTS

⅓ cup honey

2 cups quick cook
gluten-free oatmeal

¼ cup wheat germ (substitute flax
seed to make it gluten-free)

1 cup roasted chopped peanuts
(or other favorite nuts)

⅓ cup coconut crystals

¼ cup coconut oil

2 tablespoons water

½ teaspoon sea salt

1 teaspoon pure vanilla

INSTRUCTIONS

1. Preheat oven to 250°F and lightly grease a baking sheet.

2. Combine oatmeal, wheat germ, and peanuts in a large mixing bowl.

3. Combine honey, coconut crystals, coconut oil water, salt, and vanilla in a medium mixing bowl. Stir.

4. Coat oatmeal mixture with honey mixture and mix well.

5. Bake for 45-60 minutes, stirring every 10-15 minutes. Remove and cool.

6. Store in an airtight container.

MIXED BERRY WAFFLE SANDWICH

....

Looking to make something special for breakfast?
This recipe is sure to please a crowd.

....

Total Time: 15-30 minutes

Servings: 4

INGREDIENTS

1 ½ cups fresh berries

1 tablespoon butter

⅓ cup honey

8 frozen gluten-free waffles, toasted

INSTRUCTIONS

1. Blend ½ cup of berries in a blender (or food processor) and set aside.

2. Melt butter in a small saucepan over medium heat.

3. Add honey and bring to a boil.

4. Simmer 2 to 3 minutes and add berry mixture. Continue to simmer 2 to 3 minutes until syrup thickens a bit. Set this aside and keep warm.

5. Serve with 2 waffles on each plate. Top with ¼ cup fresh berries and drizzle with syrup.

SUPER SWEET POTATO CHIPS

....

Need a salty and slightly sweet snack?
These potato chips are a great way to nix the craving.

....

Total Time: 25 minutes

Servings: 3-5

INGREDIENTS

2 sweet potatoes

2 tablespoons melted butter

2 tablespoons honey

½ teaspoon ground cinnamon

Sea salt and pepper to taste

INSTRUCTIONS

1. Preheat oven to 400°F.

2. Slice sweet potatoes thinly — use a mandoline or food processor.

3. Combine honey and butter in a small bowl and toss with the potatoes to coat.

4. Line a baking pan with a silicone mat and place potatoes on mat.

5. Bake the chips for 5 minutes per side.

6. Sprinkle with cinnamon, sea salt, and pepper to taste.

OVER-THE-TOP HONEY ORANGE MARMALADE

This delicious marmalade makes a perfectly sweet topping for toast or crackers and works beautifully as a garnish for poultry or pork.

Total Time: 15-20 minutes

Servings: Variable

INGREDIENTS

2 oranges, peeled

1 jalapeno pepper

8 ounces honey

INSTRUCTIONS

1. Grate orange peels into a small pan.

2. Add honey and mix.

3. Cut pepper into small and thin sections, including seeds.

4. Place pan on medium heat and stir constantly — do not allow mixture to boil.

5. When mixture is blended and hot, put it into a clean jam jar.

6. Allow mixture to cool. No need to refrigerate.

CHOCOLATE AND COCONUT-COVERED ALMONDS

These almonds make a perfect afternoon pick-me-up.

Total Time: 45 minutes

Servings: 2-3

INGREDIENTS

1 ½ cups raw almonds

¼ cup coconut butter

1 ½ tablespoons unrefined coconut oil

2 tablespoons honey

4 ounces unsweetened baking cocoa

½ teaspoons pure vanilla extract

Pinch of sea salt

INSTRUCTIONS

1. Line a glass 9x13 pan with parchment paper.

2. Place all ingredients except almonds in a double boiler.

3. Mix and stir until mixture begins to boil.

4. Add almonds and remove mixture from heat.

5. Pour almonds in the pan, then place in the freezer for 20 minutes.

6. Store in the fridge.

HONEY-SMACKED PARFAIT

....

This parfait is a perfect mix of fresh fruit and honey.
Enjoy for breakfast, dessert, or as a snack anytime.

....

Total Time: 5 minutes

Servings: 1

INGREDIENTS

1 cup plain Greek yogurt

¼ cup honey

1 cup granola (gluten-free)

1 ½ cups strawberries, sliced

1 banana, sliced

1 ½ cups raspberries

½ cup blackberries

INSTRUCTIONS

1. Mix yogurt and honey together, then pour into a glass.

2. Alternate layers of granola, fruit, honey, and yogurt until glass is full.

3. Top with more fruit and drizzle with honey.

MELT-IN-YOUR-MOUTH HONEY BREAD

Pair this bread with your favorite bowl of soup or drizzle it with honey for a delicious snack.

Total Time: Approx. 2 hours

Servings: 1 pan

INGREDIENTS

1 ¾ cups all-purpose
gluten-free flour

6 tablespoons cornstarch

1 teaspoons xanthan gum

1 ½ teaspoons baking powder

¾ teaspoons salt

½ teaspoons baking soda

½ teaspoons coconut crystals

6 tablespoons coconut oil, melted

½ cup honey

1 teaspoons pure vanilla extract

½ cup milk, room temperature

3 tablespoons plain yogurt

3 eggs, room temperature

INSTRUCTIONS

1. Preheat oven to 350°F and grease a 9x5 pan.

2. Place flour, cornstarch, xanthan gum, baking powder, baking soda, salt and sugar in a bowl.

3. Whisk to combine with a handheld whisk.

4. Create a well in the center of the dry ingredients and add coconut oil.

5. Combine using the paddle attachment.

6. Add honey, vanilla, milk, yogurt, and eggs. Mix together after adding each ingredient. The batter should be smooth and pourable.

7. Transfer batter to prepared pan and shake it back and forth to smooth it into an even layer.

8. Bake in the center of the oven for 45 minutes.

9. Cover the bread loosely with aluminum foil. Bake until the top of the loaf springs back when lightly touched.

10. Cool for 20 minutes before transferring to a metal rack.

HONEY LOVE CINNAMON BUTTER

*Enjoy this butter on your favorite gluten-free
bread or as a fruit dip.*

Total Time: 5 minutes

Servings: Variable

INGREDIENTS

¼ cup soft butter

¼ cup honey

¼ teaspoon cinnamon powder

1 tablespoon cream cheese

INSTRUCTIONS

1. Cream the ingredients together in a bowl until they are well mixed.

SWEET AND SPICY BUTTER

....

This butter pairs well with gluten-free bread or even as a sweet and spicy topping for your favorite veggies.

....

Total Time: 5 minutes

Servings: Variable

INGREDIENTS

2 sticks unsalted butter, room temperature

2 tablespoons honey

1 tablespoons sea salt

1 habanero chili, seeded and finely diced

1 clove garlic, finely diced

INSTRUCTIONS

1. Whisk all ingredients together.

2. Chill before use.

MEDIUM HOT HONEY MANGO SALSA

Everything tastes better, hotter, and sweeter with a little mango honey salsa!

Total Time: 45 minutes

Servings: Variable

INGREDIENTS

1 large ripe mango, peeled and chopped

¼ cup red bell pepper, chopped finely

¼ cup red onion, chopped finely

2 tablespoons cilantro, chopped

2 tablespoons fresh lime juice

2 tablespoons honey

1 small jalapeno pepper, seeded and minced

2 tablespoons hot sauce

INSTRUCTIONS

1. Combine all ingredients in a large bowl.

2. Chill for about 30 minutes before serving.

HONEY-INFUSED BAKED BEANS

*Get ready for your summer barbecue with these
sweet and spicy baked beans.*

Total Time: 1 hour

Servings: 8-10

INGREDIENTS

½ cup chopped onion

4 ½ cups white beans, cooked

½ cup honey

1 tablespoon prepared mustard

1 tablespoon Worcestershire sauce

INSTRUCTIONS

1. Preheat oven to 350°F.

2. Sauté onions until tender.

3. Combine with other ingredients in a shallow 2-quart oven-safe baking dish.

4. Cover with a lid and bake for 30 minutes.

5. Uncover and bake for another 20-30 minutes.

COCONUT HONEY CHICKPEA CURRY

The taste of India has arrived in your kitchen with this delicious coconut and honey-infused chickpea curry.

Total Time: 45 minutes

Servings: 4-6

INGREDIENTS

2 tablespoons olive oil

1 onion, chopped

2 teaspoons curry powder

2 cloves garlic, mashed

1 cup vegetable stock

2 cans chickpeas

1 can coconut milk

2 tablespoons honey

1 tablespoons Sriracha
or other chili sauce

Salt and pepper to taste

Chopped cilantro, green onion,
or chives for garnish

INSTRUCTIONS

1. Heat olive oil in a large pan over medium heat.

2. Add onions, salt, and pepper and cook until onions are lightly caramelized, about 10 minutes

3. Add curry powder and garlic and stir for 20-30 seconds.

4. Add the broth and stir well to incorporate the onion mixture.

5. Add chickpeas, coconut milk, honey, and chili sauce.

6. Bring to a soft boil, then reduce heat and simmer for 15 minutes.

7. Adjust seasonings to taste.

8. Garnish with cilantro, green onion, or chives.

9. Serve over rice or grains or with warm naan bread.

SPINACH AND FRUIT HONEY SALAD

*A perfect summer salad. Slightly fruity and sweet,
this light salad is a perfect addition to an outdoor meal.*

Total Time: 15 minutes

Servings: 1-2

INGREDIENTS

SALAD

6 ounces fresh spinach

1 cup fresh strawberries, quartered

½ cup red onion, sliced thinly

½ cup fresh blueberries

¼ cup feta cheese, crumbled

DRESSING

⅓ cup balsamic vinegar

2 tablespoons honey

½ teaspoon sea salt

½ teaspoon black pepper

⅔ cup extra virgin olive oil

INSTRUCTIONS

1. Toss salad ingredients.

2. Combine dressing ingredients and mix well.

3. Drizzle salad with dressing.

HONEY CARROT
GINGER SOUP

*This smooth and satisfying soup will tantalize your taste buds.
It has just enough ginger to give it a pleasant zip.*

Total Time: 1 hour

Servings: 4-6

INGREDIENTS

2 cups baby (or adult) carrots

5 cups vegetable stock

¼ cup honey

3 garlic cloves, crushed

Pinch of sea salt

Pinch of black pepper

1 teaspoon ground ginger

½ cup Greek yogurt

Chopped parsley

INSTRUCTIONS

1. Slice carrots and put them in a saucepan with the vegetable stock, honey, garlic, salt, pepper, and ginger.

2. Bring mixture to a boil, reduce heat, and simmer for about 30 minutes, or until the carrots are soft.

3. Puree the soup in a blender and reheat before stirring in yogurt.

4. Add chopped parsley on top to garnish before serving.

CREAMY PEANUT SOUP WITH HONEY WHIPPED CREAM

The honey whipped cream on top of this unusual and delicious soup gives it just the right amount of sweetness.

Total Time: 2 hours

Servings: 4-6

INGREDIENTS

2 heads garlic

5 tablespoons olive oil

1 ½ cups peanuts,
unsalted and dry roasted

2 yellow onions, sliced

3 celery stalks, thinly sliced

¼ cup green onion
or chives, chopped

2 tablespoons unsalted butter

2 quarts vegetable broth

1 bay leaf

1 yellow potato, cut into
¼-inch cubes

¾ cup heavy cream, chilled (used
in both the soup and the topping)

Pinch of sea salt

2 tablespoons honey

1 teaspoon toasted sesame oil

INSTRUCTIONS

SOUP

1. Preheat oven to 450°F.

2. Slice off and discard one third from the top of each head of garlic and place on sheet of foil.

3. Drizzle with 2 tablespoons of olive oil and wrap the foil around the garlic.

4. Place on a baking sheet and roast until soft (about 45 minutes).

5. Let garlic cool and squeeze cloves into a small bowl. Add any oil left in foil.

6. Chop peanuts in a food processor and transfer ¼ cup to a small bowl.

7. Continue to pulse the remaining peanuts into a smooth butter. This should take about 2 minutes and will make about 2/3 cup peanut butter.

8. In a stock pot over medium heat, add onions, celery, butter and reserved garlic with oil. Stir often until celery and onions is soft, about 10-15 minutes.

9. Add broth and bay leaf. Bring to a boil.

10. Add potato and simmer until soft, about 20 minutes. Remove from heat.

11. Puree soup in a blender a little at a time. Add peanut butter with the last batch.

12. Pour soup through a strainer into a large bowl.

13. Whisk in ¼ cup of cream.

WHIPPED CREAM TOPPING

1. Add the remaining ½ cup of cream and a pinch of sea salt to a small bowl and whisk until soft cream begins to thicken into soft peaks.

2. Gradually add honey and sesame oil and continue to whisk until peaks are stiff.

3. Serve the soup with a dollop of honey whipped cream.

4. Sprinkle with chopped peanuts and chopped green onion or chives.

NOODLE-FREE PAD THAI

This light and delicious dish uses raw vegetables in place of rice.
This is a perfect gluten-free, plant based meal.

Total Time: 35 minutes

Servings: 6-8

INGREDIENTS

PAD THAI

4 medium carrots, peeled

½ pound zucchini

½ pound bean sprouts

4 onions, finely sliced

12 to 14 ounces organic extra firm tofu, drained and gently squeezed

1 small handful of chopped cilantro leaves

2 tablespoons sesame seeds

4 small wedges of lime

SAUCE

½ cup peanut butter (or almond butter)

¼ cup lime juice

2 tablespoons tamari, soy sauce, or liquid aminos

2 tablespoons honey

2 teaspoons grated ginger

Pinch of red pepper

3 tablespoons water

INSTRUCTIONS

1. Use a spiralizer or peeler to create "noodles" out of carrots and zucchini.

2. Place noodles in a large serving bowl. Add the bean sprouts, onions, chopped cilantro, and sesame seeds.

3. Slice tofu into small squares and transfer to the bowl.

4. To make the sauce, whisk together all of the ingredients until smooth and creamy.

5. Use your hands to toss the mixture and drizzle with dressing.

6. Serve with a wedge of lime.

SAVORY HONEY AND GINGER GLAZED SALMON

*This delicious broiled salmon has a tasty balance
between honey and ginger. Serve with brown rice and a salad
for a well-balanced meal.*

Total Time: 30 minutes

Servings: 4

INGREDIENTS

1 pound wild salmon fillet, cut into 4 pieces

1 scallion, minced

2 tablespoons tamari, soy sauce, or liquid aminos

1 tablespoon rice vinegar

1 tablespoon honey

1 teaspoon fresh ginger, minced

1 teaspoon toasted sesame seeds

INSTRUCTIONS

1. Preheat broiler. Line a small baking pan with foil and coat with cooking spray.

2. Whisk scallion, tamari, soy sauce or liquid aminos, honey, and ginger in a medium bowl until honey dissolves.

3. Place salmon in a zip-top bag and add 3 tablespoons of glaze. Marinate in the refrigerator for 15 minutes. Set remaining glaze aside.

4. Place salmon on baking pan, skin side down.

5. Broil 6 inches from heat source until cooked through, about 10 minutes.

6. Drizzle with remaining glaze and sesame seeds.

HONEY GLAZED ROASTED VEGETABLE SALAD

*This salad is a meal in itself, but it also
pairs nicely with poultry or fish.*

Total Time: 1 hour

Servings: 4-6

INGREDIENTS

1 medium yellow onion,
cut into 8 wedges

½ pound yams,
cut into 1-inch chunks

½ pound small red thin-skinned
potatoes, cut in half

1 red bell pepper,
cut into 1-inch chunks

4 tablespoons extra virgin olive oil

1 teaspoon sea salt

1 teaspoon pepper

½ cup coarsely chopped walnuts

2 tablespoons red wine vinegar

3 tablespoons honey

6 ounces mixed salad greens

INSTRUCTIONS

1. Preheat oven to 425°F.

2. Toss the onion, sweet potatoes, and bell pepper in a large bowl along with 3 tablespoons of oil and ½ teaspoon each of salt and pepper.

3. Place vegetables on a baking sheet. Roast until they are tender, about 40 minutes. Turn halfway through the baking time.

4. About 10 minutes before they are done, sprinkle walnuts on veggies.

5. Let vegetables cool for about 5 minutes and transfer to a large bowl.

6. Whisk together 1 tablespoon oil, vinegar, honey, and ½ teaspoon each of salt and pepper.

7. Toss greens in a large bowl along with a quarter of the dressing.

8. Place veggies on top, then drizzle remaining dressing.

HONEY 'N' LIME FISH TACOS

*Fish tacos are one of the world's most perfect foods...
and this recipe with a honey cilantro slaw does them just right!*

Total Time: 30 minutes
Servings: 6-8

INGREDIENTS

FOR THE FISH:

1 ½ pounds halibut, mahi-mahi, or cod

1 tablespoon olive oil

1 teaspoon chili powder

1 teaspoon cumin

½ teaspoon garlic powder

½ teaspoon onion powder

½ teaspoon Mexican oregano

½ teaspoon salt

FOR THE SLAW:

4 cups shredded green and/or purple cabbage

¼ cup cilantro

2 tablespoons lime juice

1 tablespoons honey

¼ teaspoon salt

¼ teaspoon black pepper

TO SERVE:

Corn tortillas

Avocado slices (or guacamole)

Salsa

Fresh cilantro

INSTRUCTIONS

First , prepare the slaw.
Then, prepare the fish.
Then, assemble your tacos.

FOR THE SLAW:

1. Combine shredded cabbage, cilantro, and lime juice in a large bowl.

2. Mix well, then add honey, salt, and pepper.

3. Stir to combine well and season to taste.

4. Add additional lime juice, honey, salt, or seasonings to taste.

5. Set aside to marinate. The salt and lime juice will soften the cabbage while you prepare the fish.

FOR THE FISH:

1. Combine the spices and salt in a small bowl.

2. Pat fish fillets dry with a paper towel and place in a container with a secure lid or a zip-top bag.

3. Add seasoning mix and shake to coat evenly.

4. Heat oil in a skillet over medium to high heat.

5. Add fish, making sure not to crowd the pan.

6. Cook for 3-4 minutes on each side until fish is cooked through.

ASSEMBLE THE TACOS:

1. Simply spoon slaw and fish into corn tortillas. Add your extras like avocado slices, guacamole, salsa, hot sauce, or fresh cilantro. Enjoy!

HONEY SESAME GLAZED TEMPEH

Tempeh is a traditional plant-based protein source that does not get anywhere near enough attention. This recipe puts tempeh in the spotlight... and it shines!

Total Time: 20 minutes

Servings: 2-3

INGREDIENTS

2 tablespoons olive oil

1 teaspoons toasted sesame oil

**8 ounces tempeh,
cut into bite-sized pieces**

¼ cup honey

¼ cup orange juice

**1 tablespoons tamari, soy sauce,
or liquid aminos**

1 tablespoon ginger, grated

**2 tablespoons sesame seeds,
toasted**

INSTRUCTIONS

1. Heat olive and sesame oil in a large pan over medium heat.

2. Add tempeh and cook until browned, stirring frequently.

3. Reduce heat if you see smoke.

4. Add orange juice, honey, soy sauce, and ginger and bring to a soft boil.

5. Simmer until liquid has thickened to a glaze, about 10 minutes.

6. Continue to turn tempeh to coat all sides and prevent sticking or burning.

7. Remove tempeh from pan and sprinkle with sesame seeds.

8. Serve over rice or other grain along with a pile of roasted vegetables!

HONEY SPICED
BLACK BEAN CHILI

*This new twist on an old time favorite
will reignite your love of chili.*

Total Time: 45 minutes

Servings: 8-10

INGREDIENTS

1 cup Vidalia onion, chopped

¼ cup garlic, chopped

½ cup green pepper, chopped

1 ½ jalapeno peppers, diced

3 cans black beans

2 cans diced tomatoes

1 teaspoons chili powder

1 teaspoons cumin

1 teaspoons thyme

½ teaspoons sea salt

½ teaspoons cinnamon

¼ cup honey

Brown rice (or cornbread)

INSTRUCTIONS

1. Sauté onion and green pepper in a stock pot with a little olive oil.

2. Cook until onion is translucent.

3. Add tomatoes, garlic, jalapenos, beans, chili powder, cumin, thyme, salt, and cinnamon.

4. Stir and simmer on low for 25 minutes.

5. Add honey and stir.

6. Serve over brown rice or with cornbread.

SWEET AND STICKY SHRIMP

Even though this meal takes only 30 minutes to make, you'll impress your family or your guests because they'll feel like they are eating at a gourmet restaurant.

Total Time: 30 minutes

Servings: 3-4

INGREDIENTS

½ cup honey

¼ cup tamari, soy sauce
or liquid aminos

3 cloves garlic, minced

1 small lemon, juiced

1 pound large shrimp,
peeled and cleaned

2 tablespoons butter

Green onions, chopped

Jasmine rice

INSTRUCTIONS

1. Whisk honey, tamari, soy sauce or liquid aminos, garlic, and lemon together in a small bowl. Add half of the sauce to the shrimp and let it marinate for 30 minutes.

2. Add butter to a skillet and melt. Add shrimp and discard the marinade. Season with salt and pepper.

3. Turn to medium high and cook until shrimp are pink, about 2 minutes each side.

4. Add reserved marinade to shrimp and cook until sauce thickens.

5. Serve with green onion garnish over a bed of jasmine rice.

GLAZED HONEY CARROTS

*This dish is a healthy side to any meal,
or it can be enjoyed on its own.*

Total Time: 35 minutes

Servings: 6-8

INGREDIENTS

3 bunches carrots, peeled

2 tablespoons unsalted butter

2 tablespoons honey

Pinch of sea salt

1 teaspoon ground ginger

1 teaspoon grated orange zest

½ cup fresh orange juice

½ teaspoon black pepper

½ teaspoon cinnamon

INSTRUCTIONS

1. Cut carrots diagonally into 1-inch slices.

2. Combine ½ cup water, butter, honey, salt, and ginger in a pan and bring to a boil.

3. Add carrots and cover the pan. Simmer over medium-low heat for 5 minutes.

4. Remove the lid and cook until water is gone.

5. Add orange zest and orange juice to the pan and toss with carrots. Simmer uncovered for 5 minutes.

6. Add pepper and cinnamon, then serve warm.

TROPICAL TWIST
FRUIT SALAD

*You will feel like you're on the islands without ever having to
leave your home with this refreshing salad.*

Total Time: 15 minutes

Servings: 6-8

INGREDIENTS

2 cups fresh blueberries

2 cups fresh raspberries

1 mango, cubed

½ fresh pineapple, cubed

½ seedless watermelon, cubed

½ cup honey

1 lime, juiced

1 orange, juiced

½ cup sliced almonds

½ cup coconut flakes, unsweetened

Fresh mint leaves

INSTRUCTIONS

1. Mix fruit together in a large bowl.

2. Whisk honey, lime juice, and orange juice together.

3. Drizzle mixture over fruit and lightly toss with coconut and almonds.

4. Serve chilled with mint leaves for garnish.

HONEYED CORN

....

*This dish will add drama and deliciousness
to any summer barbecue.*

....

Total Time: 15 minutes

Servings: 6-8

INGREDIENTS

6 ears corn

1 tablespoon butter

3 tablespoons shallots, diced

1 teaspoon sea salt

1 teaspoon black pepper

¼ teaspoon red pepper flakes

2 tablespoons honey

½ tablespoon apple cider vinegar

INSTRUCTIONS

1. Cut corn off the cob and sauté with butter.

2. Cook shallots until they are translucent.

3. Mix corn and shallots, then add salt and pepper. Cook until corn is tender.

4. Whisk honey, apple cider vinegar and red pepper flakes in a bowl.

5. Combine with corn and cook for a few minutes until well mixed.

GARLIC AND HONEY
EGGS SUPREME

*It is said that Albert Einstein like his eggs with honey...
so there must be something to it! If you are looking for a new
and tasty breakfast dish, this one is for you!*

Total Time: 10 minutes

Servings: 2

INGREDIENTS

2 large eggs (double or triple if serving more than 2)

1 teaspoon honey

Dash of garlic powder

Pinch of nutmeg

Pinch of cinnamon

Pinch of allspice

Sea salt and black pepper

Coconut oil

INSTRUCTIONS

1. Whisk the ingredients together in a bowl.

2. Cook in skillet with coconut oil until done.

HONEY KISSED
COUSCOUS SALAD

....

*Filling enough to be eaten as a meal, this delicious and naturally
sweet salad also makes an excellent side.*

....

Total Time: 20 minutes

Servings: 4-6

INGREDIENTS

4 cups water

1 ½ cups couscous

1 ½ tablespoons coconut oil

2 English cucumbers, peeled and diced

1 red pepper, diced

1 green onion, diced

Sea salt and black pepper

¼ cup honey

¼ cup apple cider vinegar

½ cup olive oil

½ cup raisins

½ cup almonds

Fresh baby greens

INSTRUCTIONS

1. Bring water and 1 teaspoon salt to a boil.

2. Add couscous and return to a boil. Cook for 2 minutes.

3. Remove from heat and cover. Let stand for 3 minutes.

4. Heat honey and vinegar in a small pan until warm. Whisk in olive oil and season with salt and pepper.

5. Add raisins, chopped veggies and almonds to couscous and fluff with a fork.

6. Drizzle with dressing. Serve warm or chilled over baby greens.

WELCOME HOME APPLE CHERRY COMPOTE

Nothing says "welcome home" better than this delicious fruit compote.

Total Time: 1 hour

Servings: 6-8

INGREDIENTS

CRUST

3 cups rolled gluten-free oats

½ cup coconut crystals

½ teaspoons pumpkin pie spice

2 teaspoons baking powder

½ teaspoon sea salt

1 cup whole milk
or non-dairy alternative

2 eggs

½ cup honey

1 teaspoon pure vanilla

½ cup melted butter

COMPOTE

2 tart apples, peeled and diced into ½-inch pieces

½ cup dried cherries

⅓ cup honey

½ cup apple juice

1 orange, juiced and zested

2 tablespoons butter

1 teaspoon pure vanilla

INSTRUCTIONS

1. Preheat oven to 350°F and grease an 8x8 pan with coconut oil.

2. Mix the oats, coconut crystals, pumpkin pie spice, baking powder, and salt in a large bowl.

3. Whisk the milk, eggs, honey, and vanilla in another bowl.

4. Combine the wet and dry ingredients and add the melted butter. Mix well.

5. Spread the mixture in the pan and bake for 25 to 30 minutes.

6. While the oats are baking, combine the apples, cherries, honey, apple juice, and orange juice together in a small saucepan.

7. Allow the mixture to boil for 1 minute. Reduce heat and simmer for 15 minutes. Keep stirring.

8. Remove the compote from the heat and stir in the orange zest, vanilla, and butter.

9. Allow the oats to cool for 10 minutes and pour compote mixture on top.

BLUEBERRY AND HONEY BREAKFAST CAKE

*This moist breakfast cake is loaded with blueberries,
one of the most nutrient-dense foods on the planet.*

Total Time: 1 hour, 30 minutes

Servings: 1 cake

INGREDIENTS

2 cups fresh blueberries

½ cup honey

2 tablespoons fresh lemon juice

1 ½ cups gluten-free baking flour

2 teaspoons baking powder

½ teaspoon salt

2 eggs

¼ cup milk

2 tablespoons fresh lemon juice

1 teaspoon freshly grated lemon peel

1 teaspoon pure vanilla

6 tablespoons melted butter

½ teaspoon baking soda

INSTRUCTIONS

1. Preheat oven to 350°F and grease a 9-inch round pan with coconut oil.

2. Add a thin layer of cornmeal, then blueberries.

3. Sprinkle the blueberries with flour, drizzle with honey and lemon juice. Set this aside.

4. In a small mixing bowl, combine flour, baking powder, baking soda, and salt. Set this aside.

5. In a medium mixing bowl, combine eggs, honey, milk, lemon juice, lemon peel, and vanilla. Beat with a fork until well blended.

6. Add the flour mixture and mix well.

7. Stir in the melted butter and mix.

8. Pour batter over the blueberries and spread evenly.

9. Bake for 30 to 35 minutes or until a toothpick inserted in the center comes out clean.

10. Cool for 10 minutes on a wire rack.

TROPICAL SORBET

*After a warm day outdoors, nothing will cool you down
in a sweeter fashion than this refreshing home-made
honey sweetened sorbet.*

Total Time: 10 minutes, plus several hours freezing time

Servings: 8-10

INGREDIENTS

3 cups orange juice

1 ⅔ cups frozen mango pieces

1 ⅔ cups pineapple chunks

¾ cup honey

⅓ cup fresh lime juice

INSTRUCTIONS

1. Blend 1 ½ cups of orange juice and remaining ingredients.

2. Stir in the remaining orange juice.

3. Freeze until smooth and creamy.

PASSION FRUIT CUPCAKES

Passion fruit and blueberries give these cupcakes just the right amount of tart fruity goodness.

Total Time: 1 hour

Servings: about 18 cupcakes

STEP ONE: CUPCAKES

INGREDIENTS

2 cups all-purpose gluten-free flour

½ teaspoons baking soda

½ teaspoons salt

¾ cup passion fruit nectar

¼ cup buttermilk

½ cup butter, softened

½ cup honey

2 large eggs

1 cup fresh blueberries

INSTRUCTIONS

1. Sift together flour, baking soda, baking powder, and salt. Set aside.

2. In a glass measuring bowl, cream butter until it becomes fluffy.

3. Add honey and mix well.

4. Add eggs one at a time and mix. Then add buttermilk and passion fruit nectar.

5. Add half of the dry ingredients to the butter. Mix on low with hand mixer until well combined.

6. Add remaining dry ingredients until combined.

7. Fold in blueberries.

8. Fill paper-lined muffin tins 2/3 full.

9. Bake for 18 to 22 minutes or until a toothpick inserted in the center of a cupcake comes out clean.

10. Cool cupcakes for 10 minutes.

STEP TWO: WHIPPED CREAM

INGREDIENTS

1 cup heavy whipping cream

1 tablespoon honey

2 tablespoons passion fruit nectar

INSTRUCTIONS

1. Combine whipping cream, honey, and passion nectar in a mixing bowl.

2. Beat until peaks form.

CARROT CAKE TO DIE FOR

You have never tasted a carrot cake like this one.
You'll never need another carrot cake recipe again!

Total Time: 1 hour, plus 3 hours cooling time

Servings: 2 loaves

INGREDIENTS

3 cups blanched almond flour

1 teaspoon sea salt

1 teaspoon baking soda

1 teaspoon ground cinnamon

1 teaspoon ground nutmeg

5 large eggs

½ cup honey

¼ cup grapeseed oil

3 cups carrots, grated

1 cup raisins

1 cup walnuts

INSTRUCTIONS

1. Preheat oven to 325°F. Lightly grease a pair of 9-inch cake pans with coconut oil.

2. Mix the almond flour, salt, baking soda, cinnamon, and nutmeg in a large bowl.

3. In a medium bowl, mix together eggs, honey, and oil.

4. Stir carrots, raisins, and walnuts into wet ingredients.

5. Stir wet into dry ingredients.

6. Transfer batter into greased pans.

7. Bake for 35 minutes.

8. Cool each cake for 3 hours, then remove from pan.

9. Frost with your favorite cream cheese or butter cream frosting.

DAIRY-FREE HONEY COOKIES

If you like crispy on the outside and chewy on the inside, these cookies are for you.

Total Time: 20 minutes

Servings: 18-24 cookies

INGREDIENTS

½ cup plus 2 tablespoons light extra virgin olive oil

⅔ cup sugar

¼ cup honey

1 large egg

1 teaspoon pure vanilla

2 cups gluten-free flour

2 teaspoons baking soda

½ teaspoon baking powder

¼ teaspoon salt

⅓ cup turbinado sugar

INSTRUCTIONS

1. Preheat oven to 375°F. Line a cookie sheet with parchment paper.

2. Combine olive oil, sugar, and honey in a large mixing bowl. Mix until combined.

3. Add egg and vanilla to mixture. Mix until combined and sugar dissolves.

4. In a separate bowl, blend flour and salt together with a fork. Be sure there are no lumps.

5. Add flour and salt mixture to wet mixture and blend until combined.

6. Shape 1 tablespoon of cookie dough into a ball and roll it in the turbinado sugar. Place cookies 2 ½ inches apart on cookie sheet. Bake for 8 minutes.

7. Cool completely on a cooling rack before eating.

NO-BAKE PEANUT BUTTER CHOCOLATE BARS

....

This is the perfect high protein, high fiber sweet treat.
The ratio of peanut butter to chocolate in these bars is perfection.
We dare you to eat just one.

....

Total Time: 30 mins plus 2 hours chilling time (or overnight)

Servings: about 24 bars

INGREDIENTS

2 cups natural peanut butter

¾ cup butter, softened

¾ cup gluten-free oat bran

½ cup honey

4 cups gluten-free graham crackers, crushed

2 cups mini dark chocolate chips

STEP ONE: BOTTOM LAYER

INSTRUCTIONS

1. Lightly grease a 13x9 glass pan.

2. Combine 1 ¼ peanut butter and honey in a large bowl until creamy.

3. Mix the oat bran, graham cracker crumbs and ½ cup dark chocolate chips.

4. Use a spatula to press down mixture evenly into the baking pan.

STEP TWO: TOP LAYER

INSTRUCTIONS

1. Melt ¾ cup peanut butter and 1 ½ cups of dark chocolate chips over low heat. Use a heavy bottom pot and stir until smooth.

2. Spread the peanut butter mixture over the bottom layer and refrigerate at least 2 hours. It's best to leave it overnight or until firm.

3. Cut into bars. Store in refrigerator.

LIGHT STRAWBERRY AND KIWI CRUMBLE

This sweet treat is perfect for those watching their waistline — and it doesn't skimp on flavor, either.

Total Time: 1 hour plus 3 hours chilling time

Servings: 6-8

STEP ONE: CRUST

INGREDIENTS

1 ½ cups walnuts

10 dates

1 tablespoon coconut oil

½ teaspoon baking soda

Pinch of sea salt

INSTRUCTIONS

1. In a food processor, pulse the walnuts until they are smaller than pea size, but not quite a powder.

2. Add dates and pulse to chop.

3. Add coconut oil, baking soda, and salt. Process until it is a smooth consistency.

4. Scoop batter and place it into a glass pie pan.

5. Use your hands to mold the batter into the pan and up along the sides.

6. Bake for 12 minutes or until the edges turn brown.

7. Once cool, lay the strawberries and kiwis in the crust. They should come to just below the crust line.

STEP TWO: FILLING

INGREDIENTS

½ cup fresh strawberries

½ cup water

2 teaspoons pure vanilla

2 tablespoons honey

3 envelopes unflavored gelatin

3/4 cup kiwi, chopped

1 ¼ cup fresh strawberries, chopped

INSTRUCTIONS

1. Add first five ingredients into a blender and blend until pureed.

2. Pour into a saucepan and bring to a boil.

3. Reduce heat to a low, rolling boil and whisk for 5 minutes.

4. Once the liquid mixture is done, pour it over the fruit.

5. Cover and place in refrigerator to chill. It should take about 3 hours to firm up.

CHEWY CHOCOLATE
CHIP COOKIES

*Gooey goodness says it all about this delectable chocolate treats.
Have a napkin ready!*

Total Time: 30 minutes

Servings: about 18 cookies

INGREDIENTS

1 ¾ cup almond flour

¼ cup honey

¾ cup mini dark chocolate chips

¼ tablespoon coconut oil

¼ teaspoon sea salt

¼ teaspoon baking soda

1 teaspoon pure vanilla

INSTRUCTIONS

1. Preheat oven to 350°F and line a cookie sheet with parchment paper.

2. Combine all ingredients in a mixing bowl except the chocolate chips.

3. Fold in chocolate chips.

4. Scoop out dough by tablespoon and place on cookie sheet, 3 inches apart.

5. Press each cookie lightly with a fork.

6. Bake for 6 to 10 minutes or until brown — do not overcook.

7. Cool for 10 minutes before eating.

SWEET CRUSTLESS APPLE PIE

Pair this apple pie with a piece of cheddar cheese for a great-tasting combo. You won't miss the crust at all!

Total Time: 1 hour

Servings: 4-6

INGREDIENTS

5 cups apples, peeled and cut

1 teaspoons cinnamon

2 tablespoons coconut crystals

¾ cup melted butter

½ cup honey

1 cup gluten-free flour

½ teaspoon xanthan gum

1 large brown egg

Pinch of sea salt

INSTRUCTIONS

1. Preheat oven to 350°F and grease a deep dish pie pan.

2. Place apples in pan, sprinkle with cinnamon and 1 tablespoon coconut crystals.

3. Mix melted butter, honey, flour, and xanthan gum together.

4. Pour over apples and spread with a spatula.

5. Sprinkle more cinnamon and the rest of the coconut crystals over the apples.

6. Bake for 45 minutes.

SALTED HONEY ICE CREAM

This ice cream is so easy to make and does not require an ice cream maker. The whole family will enjoy this special treat.

Total Time: 30 minutes plus 6 hours freezing time
Servings: Variable

INGREDIENTS

2 cups heavy whipping cream

1 can sweetened condensed milk

¼ cup honey

½ teaspoon sea salt flakes

INSTRUCTIONS

1. Pour whipping cream into the bowl of a stand mixer with a whisk attachment.

2. Mix on low speed to start, then increase to high speed until stiff peaks form. This usually takes about 2 minutes.

3. Fold condensed milk into mixture with a spatula along with honey and sea salt. Continue to stir gently until combined.

4. Pour into a freezer-safe container.

5. Drizzle with honey and freeze for 6 hours.

6. Drizzle with more honey when you serve.

YUMMY HONEY FLAN

*This elegant dessert is sure to be a hit at your next dinner party.
But why save it until then? Enjoy it now!*

Total Time: 1 hour 35 minutes plus 3 hours chilling time

Servings: 6

INGREDIENTS

½ cup coconut sugar

7 tablespoons honey

1 can sweetened condensed milk

1 cup milk

3 large eggs

1 large egg yolk

¼ teaspoons sea salt

INSTRUCTIONS

1. Preheat oven to 350°F.

2. Sprinkle sugar in a 3-quart saucepan. Place over medium heat and cook gently until sugar melts and turns a light brown. Shake pan while it cooks.

3. Slowly stir in 3 tablespoons of honey.

4. Remove from heat and pour hot sugar into 6 ramekins.

5. Place condensed milk and remaining four ingredients into a blender, then process until smooth. Pour evenly into the ramekins.

6. Add 1 inch of hot tap water to the pan. Place ramekins in the pan. Cover loosely with aluminum foil.

7. Bake for 30 to 35 minutes or until lightly set. Perfect flan will jiggle slightly.

8. Remove ramekins from water bath and cool for 30 minutes. Cover and chill for 3 hours.

9. When you are ready to serve, loosen flan with a knife around the edges and serve inverted.

SCRUMPTIOUS HONEY TAFFY

....

This single-ingredient taffy is not just for kids.
Adults will love to pull and chew on this fun treat!

....

Total Time: 1 hour

Servings: 24-48 candies, depending on size

Note: You'll need a candy
thermometer for this one. .

INGREDIENTS

1 pound honey

Coconut oil cooking spray

INSTRUCTIONS

1. Line a baking sheet with parchment paper.

2. Put honey in medium saucepan and cook uncovered over medium-low heat until it begins to boil.

3. Continue cooking until your candy thermometer registers 280°F.

4. Pour the mixture into a prepared pan and spread evenly.

5. Cool for 20 minutes.

6. Spray your hands lightly with coconut oil spray.

7. Fold the honey onto itself to make a ball.

8. Stretch taffy into a long strand, fold and press ends together.

9. Stretch and fold for another 5 minutes, the taffy will change from a an amber color to a lighter tan color.

10. Wrap in plastic wrap that is also coated in coconut oil spray.

11. Chill for 10 minutes.

12. Spray a knife with coconut oil and cut taffy into 4 equal pieces.

13. Roll each piece into a 12-inch snake and cut each one into 1-2 inch pieces.

14. Wrap each piece in wax paper.

PERFECT PEACH AND HONEY POPSICLES

The creamy goodness of these popsicles are a favorite treat all summer long.

Total Time: 1 hour plus 4 hours freezing time

Servings: 8-10 popsicles

INGREDIENTS

1 pound ripe peaches, peeled and sliced into ½-inch wedges

6 tablespoons honey

Pinch of sea salt

2 cups whole Greek yogurt

1 tablespoon lemon juice

½ teaspoon pure vanilla extract

INSTRUCTIONS

1. Preheat oven to 350°F. Line a baking sheet with parchment paper.

2. Place sliced peaches on a baking sheet and toss with 2 tablespoons of honey and a dash of sea salt.

3. Arrange the peaches in a single layer.

4. Roast for 30 to 40 minutes, or until peaches are soft. Stir halfway through.

5. While peaches are roasting, combine the yogurt, ¼ cup honey, lemon juice, and vanilla extract in a medium bowl.

6. Put mixture in the refrigerator to keep cool.

7. After peaches are cool, gently fold them into the yogurt mixture.

8. Transfer the mixture to a popsicle mold and freeze for at least 4 hours.

9. When you are ready to eat them, run warm water around the molds to loosen popsicles.

ALMOND HONEY CHAI TEA

*This warm and naturally sweet drink is perfect for cuddling up
with a book on a chilly afternoon.*

Total Time: 35 minutes

Servings: 6-8

INGREDIENTS

½ **cup honey**

2 **cups water**

2 **black tea bags**

2 **teaspoons pure vanilla**

½ **teaspoons ground ginger**

½ **teaspoons ground allspice**

½ **teaspoons ground cinnamon**

INSTRUCTIONS

1. Combine honey, water, tea, vanilla, and spices in a medium pan.

2. Bring to a boil. Reduce heat and simmer for about 5 minutes.

3. Remove from heat and cover. Allow tea to steep for about 30 minutes.

4. Remove tea bags, cover, and refrigerate the base.

5. To serve this drink hot, mix equal parts of chai tea base and milk or non-dairy alternative. Heat on the stove with medium heat. To serve cold, mix equal parts of the tea base and milk (or milk substitute) over ice.

SUNSHINE FRUIT SMOOTHIE

Looking for a quick and nutritious breakfast option?
This smoothie tastes great and will keep you s
atisfied all morning long.

Total Time: 5 minutes

Servings: 1-2

INGREDIENTS

2 cups milk (or non-dairy substitute)

1 cup frozen blueberries

1 cup frozen strawberries

1 frozen banana, medium

½ scoop protein powder

1 tablespoon honey

2 tablespoons Greek yogurt

INSTRUCTIONS

1. Place all ingredients in a blender.

2. Blend until smooth. Enjoy!

SIMPLY SWEET
HOT CHOCOLATE

*Chocolate lovers will enjoy this rich and creamy
honey sweetened cocoa drink.*

Total Time: 10 minutes

Servings: 1

INGREDIENTS

**1 cup whole milk
(or non-dairy alternative)**

2 tablespoons honey

**2 tablespoons unsweetened
cocoa powder**

Pinch of sea salt

INSTRUCTIONS

1. Whisk honey, cocoa powder, and salt in pot over medium heat. Bring to simmer.

2. Whisk in milk very slowly.

3. Cook and keep stirring until slightly thick and bubbles appear at the edge.

FRUITY SUMMER SLUSH

Cool off after a day in the sun with this refreshing fruity slush.

Total Time: 5 minutes
Servings: 1-2

INGREDIENTS

1 ½ cups fresh squeezed orange juice

½ cup honey

2 tablespoons fresh lemon juice

2 tablespoons fresh lime juice

1 ½ cups frozen blueberries

1 cup crushed ice

1 lemon wedge (or lime)

INSTRUCTIONS

1. Combine orange juice, honey, lemon and lime juices in a blender. Blend until honey is dissolved.

2. Add blueberries and ice, then puree.

3. Garnish with a lemon or lime wedge.

FROTHY HONEY LATTE

*Forget that expensive coffee shop coffee and
make your own healthy drink at home.*

Total Time: 10 minutes

Servings: 1-2

INGREDIENTS

2 cups strong coffee

**1 cup whole milk
(or non-dairy alternative)**

¼ cup honey

2 cups ice

INSTRUCTIONS

1. Whisk coffee, milk and honey together until honey is dissolved.

2. Chill and blend in a blender with ice before serving.

HONEY AND APPLE CIDER VINEGAR ELIXIR

....

*This delicious drink will help boost your metabolism,
improve your immune system and increase energy.*

....

Total Time: 5 minutes

Servings: 1

INGREDIENTS

2 tablespoons honey

1 tablespoon apple cider vinegar

8 ounces cold water

INSTRUCTIONS

1. Mix honey and apple cider vinegar together in a glass.

2. Add cold water and stir to combine.

3. Drink 1 to 3 times a day before meals.

HONEY AND LEMON GREEN TEA

Curl up with a good book and a cup of this delicious, healthy tea.

Total Time: 5 minutes

Servings: 1

INGREDIENTS

1 cup water

1 green tea bag

1 tablespoon honey

1 slice lemon

INSTRUCTIONS

1. Add boiling water to cup with tea bag.

2. Allow tea to steep for 5 minutes.

3. Add lemon slice.

4. Add honey and stir.

BANANA AND COCOA TOFU SMOOTHIE

This delicious smoothie will get your day started in the right direction. The tofu makes this drink smooth and the honey gives it just the right amount of sweetness.

Total Time: 5 minutes

Servings: 1-2

INGREDIENTS

1 frozen banana

½ cup silken tofu

½ cup vanilla almond milk

2 tablespoons cocoa powder

1 tablespoon honey

INSTRUCTIONS

1. Add all ingredients into a blender.

2. Blend until smooth. Enjoy!

LUSCIOUS LAVENDER AND HONEY LEMONADE

Cool off with this herbal-infused lavender delight.

Total Time: 45 minutes

Servings: 1-2

INGREDIENTS

½ cup honey

1 tablespoon dried lavender buds

3 springs fresh lavender

1 cup fresh lemon juice

3 cups water, filtered

INSTRUCTIONS

1. Mix honey, lavender, and 3 cups of filtered water in a saucepan over medium heat.

2. Bring mixture to a boil and stir to dissolve the honey. Set aside to cool.

3. Cover and refrigerate.

4. Add lavender sprigs and lemon juice to a measuring cup and gently swish to release the oils.

5. Strain honey and lavender water. Mix it with lemon juice and let it set for about 15 minutes before removing sprigs.

6. Refrigerate for 30 minutes before serving.